An Eschatological Isolation:

a resident physician's reflections from the Coronavirus pandemic

poems by

Ammura Hernandez MD

Finishing Line Press
Georgetown, Kentucky

An Eschatological Isolation:

a resident physician's reflections from
the Coronavirus pandemic

Publisher: Leah Huete de Maines

Editor: Christen Kincaid

Cover Art: Michelle Singh

Author Photo: Michelle Singh

Cover Design: Elizabeth Maines McCleavy

Order online: www.finishinglinepress.com
also available on amazon.com

Author inquiries and mail orders:
Finishing Line Press
P. O. Box 1626
Georgetown, Kentucky 40324
U. S. A.

In honor and memory of all whose lives were affected or taken by the novel coronavirus; and to the restaurant and grocery workers, mail and delivery workers, first responders, hospital staff, and health care workers who soldiered the fight from the beginning.

Chapter 1: Entropy Bridges

March 9th, 2020

I went to sushi with Nora and Catelyn, happy to third wheel their perpetual bestfriendness. I just so happened to be sitting in front of them in class and turned around as they discussed their happy hour plans; it would've been rude not to invite me. I arrived early, they arrived together. We were the only ones in the restaurant, unusual for a DC happy hour in Dupont Circle.

"Can we order family style?" Catelyn asked to the table but looking at me.

"Of course!"

"Great! This is lowkey our favorite happy hour. The deals are wild!" She drew out the wild as though the i lasted for four syllables; long enough for the excitement to reach her eyes as they popped slightly out of their sockets.

Nora and Catelyn barely looked at the menu when the server approached us for order, and both rattled off what I presumed to be their usual favorites. They both looked at me, "Anything else?" they said in unison.

"No, I think y'all covered it!"

Catelyn launched into a lecture on SARS-CoV-2, what would become known as 2019 novel coronavirus, or COVID-19. The virus had started to spread rapidly through Wuhan, China, its place of origin marked as a food marketplace. I pictured the back alleys of Chinatown in San Francisco, with the ducks hanging in the windows, and fish sitting on ice buckets in the sidewalk.

The virus had started to spread insidiously across the world, spreading fear and wonder within the medical field. Initially, it was known as a respiratory virus, causing severe pneumonia in elderly populations. The first reports suggested alarmingly high death rates. *How infectious is this virus? How is it spread? Can we test for it? Who is at risk?*

Catelyn continued, "I've read every article, every day about this virus for the past week. I went to *both* grand rounds at the hospital. It spreads by respiratory droplets; they say such droplets can travel six feet. I's looking like the morbidity rate will be around 1% ONE PERCENT. WIIILD. Influenza has a mortality rate of 0.1% That is 100 times more deadly!" Her speech increased in speed and volume as she spoke. Like many doctors, she was impressed, amazed really, at the power a tiny microbe can hold over the human race.

With all our bells and whistles, with our modernity and pride, with our billion-dollar expenditure on healthcare, the world was about to learn just how tenuous humanity is. After four years of medical school, our hope and expectation of The Great Defining Medicine would become disillusioned in a matter of months. Chatting over sushi about a virus on the other side of the world on a misty March day, little did we know it would be the last time we saw eachother, the last time we sat in a restaurant, the last time we shared food, the last time we trusted raw fish, the last time we hugged a friend.

There was no toilet paper. Anywhere. Not online. Not in stores. We had three roles. There were no filtered masks online to order. I went to the CVS in Foggy Bottom and then to the Whole Foods. I walked through Washington Circle, admiring George, eternally frozen as he mounted his horse for a forward charge; I wondered what he thought of his city on the brink of internal isolation.

I walked to CVS in Dupont Circle, hoping they would still have overpriced hand sanitizer in stock. The isles were empty; devoid of Clorox, bleach wipes, toiled paper, and hand sanitizer. I walked to Soviet Safeway, on 17th, street only to find the same empty shelves. It seemed all of DC, the nation's capital, was completely cleared out of all essential cleaning items.

After a week of miscommunications, Dean's meetings, and a pointed collection of student criticisms written by yours truly, the School of Medicine officially pulled all medical students off of patient rotations and all classes went virtual, urging us to stay home, to "shelter in place" and conform to socially distanced practices.

Colleges and universities were amongst the first institutions to take proactive actions in limiting the spread of the newly arising pandemic. While the president continued to dismiss the threat, college presidents around the country were sending students home, closing their campuses, and transitioning their curriculums to fully online and virtual learning.

The world in its totality had entered hysteria. A word typically to be avoided due to its patriarchal and misogynistic herstory, but the emergence of COVID-19, or novel coronavirus, brought in its wake an atmosphere of uncontrollable emotional angst to the point of terror, overexaggeration, and an undertone of psychological distress manifested into physiological symptoms, or the "worried well," with an overtone of attention-seeking behavior, namely by Mr. Trump, who instead of taking presidential action, overwhelmed the American public with selfgratifying tweets and misjudgments. The world, in a word, devolved into hysteria. The Law of entropy was true: without intervention, everything tends towards chaos.

Mayor Bowser of DC, in line with mayors across the country, in accordance with guidelines from the Centers for Disease Control and Prevention (CDC), prohibited all "Mass Gatherings" of greater than 50 people, and discouraged gathering of greater than 10 people, particularly amongst those at risk individuals: people over ages 65, those with underlying conditions, immunocompromised. All non-essential stores were ordered to close. Restaurants, coffee-shops, and bars were ordered to shift from seated service to grab-and-go options exclusively.

Eddie, which was short for Edwardo, came over for dinner with his co-intern Raj, straight from the hospital. I told them we are charging for toilet paper. They laughed. *But seriously, don't use my toilet paper.* I was ashamed of my own thoughts. Eddie was my best friend, my former roommate, one of the few citizens of DC with whom I typically held no boundaries. As I let go of his welcoming embrace, I found myself worried about touching him, even though young, healthy patients were deemed low risk for complications at that time. His co-intern made loud statements about impending doom and death in an emphatic and sarcastic tone; I was joking too, but that was weeks ago. By this time, the panic was justified by mounting death tolls; the virus was spreading despite all our measures. The hysteria was suddenly reasonable. The threat was real though it seemed invisible, though people were still pretending it wasn't.

They had brought Chinese take-out, with an individual meal for each of us. It felt foreign to sit together for dinner without sharing plates.

Eventually, we migrated to the couch. Eddie sprawled across the couch, his legs resting on mine. Raj brought our four glasses to the coffee table, pouring each of us a hefty refill of wine. He sat on the carpet, his head at Eddie's knees. My partner sat in his usual spot on the leather chair, our hands resting together on his armrest. A normal scene of friends sitting intimately together now seemed like an infection train of communicable disease. We drank through the first bottle of wine. Then onto the second as we flipped through standup comedy specials on Netflix.

Our guests left, drunkenly stumbling down the hallway from our apartment. As I shut the door, I looked over at my partner, still sitting in his leather chair: calm, pensive. Catching his eye, I said hesitantly, almost a whisper, "I don't think we should have anyone over for a while…especially from the hospital…" The statement hung in the air like the sticky smell of our Chinese take-out, as I stood, still clinging to the doorknob, beginning to realize I just shut the door on a life I once knew.

My partner started sending me daily updates: 80,894 cases in China, with 3,237 deaths; 35,731 cases in Italy, with 2,978 deaths; 13,716 cases in Spain with 598 deaths; 8,413 deaths in South Korea, with 84 deaths; 8,017 cases in the US with 143 deaths.

My email flooded with information regarding COVID-19: how the hospital is responding; preserving personal protective equipment (PPE), newest treatment options, morbidity and mortality, what the school of medicine is doing, what the undergraduate school is doing etc. etc. I ignored most of them, feeling overwhelmed by the sea of panicked discourse.

I opened one email, outlining the medical student led COVID Task Force. I chuckled to myself, fully expecting a medical student task force to produce more useful content and proposals in a matter of days than the White House Coronavirus Task Force in a matter of weeks. If there is anything medical students are certainly not good at, it's *quarantining*. Medical students wanted to help. Being largely healthy and young, those without at-risk family members at home started itching to *do something*. Students created a system of at-home babysitters to provide childcare for health-care workers. Students screened calls to the ED for patients worried about their symptoms, most of whom were the "worried well" patients overcome by the anxiety of the COVID atmosphere who were low risk or not eligible to be tested. Students called and emailed family and friends and shared social media posts, spending hours disseminating trusted guidelines and dispelling unnecessary fear and fake news. When being told they were unnecessary personal, who's health the university was unwilling to risk, students made themselves necessary. Because we *needed* to be. Because we are helpful out of a fear of being disposable, and the pride found at being on the front lines of disaster. It's not *service*. Or compassion. Such virtues are about the other, but the Id and Ego are far greater. Amidst a pandemic I realized my dreams of *making a difference* were nothing but the need to have a life that mattered, to find meaning in the banal abyss of this virus-stricken, hell-bend, ice-cap melting world; as though I would have no other way to prove that I existed at all.

The National Park Services closed all roads and parking leading to the Tidal Basin to increase social distancing throughout DC, with so many tourists and locals crowding in for the cherry blossom full bloom.

Every year, the full bloom lasts about two weeks; I have always gone to visit the blossoming blossoms every day or every other day during their bloom. You could say I'm a little obsessed, but something about the blossoms just get me: the whisper sweet secrets to my soul; I feel them like my own heartbeat when I am with them; they overwhelm my capacity to understand with a soft, tiny, whimsy of breath.

The first spring bloom I missed:

Slowly with haste
Petals fall before they bloom
In essence, fleeting.

Behind closed doors,
They whispered before me
Shuddered, knowing they're all but gone.

Wilting with each passing day,
For fear of catching the dreaded disease
The blossoms and I drifted before full bloom.

But unlike me,
The blossoms bloom when they bloom
With or without an onlooking gaze.

But I still sit,
By my windowsill
Waiting, still, for my new life begin.

Young, healthy patients were starting to die from COVID-19. Healthy patients were decompensating too quickly for medical teams to respond. Young were coming in with oxygen saturations in the 70s, well below the normal of 95-100%. Young patients were being intubated, in the intensive care unit (ICU). We had thought young, healthy people were not at risk for complications, but the numbers started mounting. Suddenly *everyone* was at risk of high complication rates and intubation.

March 30th, 2020

The US reported 163,417 cases and 3,055 deaths. Italy reported 101,739 cases and 11,591 deaths. Spain reported 85,195 with 7,340 deaths. China reported 81,470 cases with 3,304 deaths. German reported 57,298 cases with 455 deaths. France reported 44,550 cases and 3,024 deaths.

Life lingered on. My partner and I fell into a slow routine. He continued to work remotely; our dining table turned into office desk. He worked in politics and voter registration. What with the constant changes to daily life, his work was exhausted by how to continue to mobilize and protect voters for the upcoming election. The final chapter of my medical school career had diminished into literature reviews and online modules, instead of the hospital rotations I had scheduled. We ate every lunch and dinner together, cooking our usual meals over and over again. We had a drink every night over a movie or TV show and slowly rounded off to bed by midnight.

Convince myself the day is worth getting out of bed for…Why? I'm not quite sure.

Kahlua in my coffee every morning because, well why not….

Work on your writing. Work on modules. Read about COVID. Read about treatments.

Read the CDC's new guidelines. Read the DC govt guidelines. Read the Contra Costa County guidelines.

Go on the Daily Walk because your body needs to move, I guess. Keep six feet from everyone.

Keep six feet apart from the neighbor out for a stroll; six feet apart from the old lady inching across the street; six feet apart from the security office at the door.

Don't touch the man on the street when you give him some dollar bills.

Meditate three minutes. Stretch twelve minutes. Breath four minutes. Don't let your mind wander.

Convince yourself it's time to go to bed though your body is not tired because nothing happened the whole of the day.

Call your parents. Skype a friend. Text your cousin.

Repeat.

I lied when I said, Never mind, it doesn't matter. Deep breath; as though My deep breath would Make it not matter.

It's been 21 days: Cooped.
Together.
It is hard to know
Which words matter.

But maybe the deep breath
Will really let it go. And maybe it really doesn't matter. And maybe I will really forget.
And maybe it wasn't a lie.

Bouncing around these four walls
With the doors locked
And windows shut,
Four walls, my brain space
It's hard to tell a lie from just the echo.

Trader Joe's started allowing only a handful of customers into the store at a time, as to maximize social distancing. We lined up behind the rest to wait our turn to enter. Blue painting tape lined the floor every six feet to remind us to keep distance even while in line. These tape lines started popping up outside most stores: Whole Foods, the City Bike Shop, Panera.

April 3rd, 2020

The CDC recommended everyone wear masks when in public places, due to increasing findings that a significant portion of individuals with coronavirus lack the symptoms can still transmit the virus. Later, the CDC published line by line directions on how to make your own mask, as though the CDC was suddenly a mommy blog. I started seeing Etsy adds for cloth mask on every platform.

I recalled a conversation with Eddie, "What do people think these masks are doing? They're not filtered. Cotton don't stop RONA!"

I made two dinky masks with scrap fabric at the bottom of my closet—navy fabric with light blue stitching—and hung them on the octopus key hook. I remembered Catelyn's enthusiasm. All the precautions are just shots in the dark. *Stay six feet apart.* Show me the data that says six feet mean anything other than a random number a group of infectious disease docs decided sounded feasible.

Clinging to masks like cotton cloth shields. Feasting on Vitamin C though we pee it all out. Spritzing EtOH mist every few minutes, like sacred swords. Fit with a full suit of empty amour, we can't even see the real parasite. Was with us all the while.

April 4th, 2020. A couple in India named their twins Corona and Covid. *Poor kids.*

Bored, bored, bored. He was pacing. I'd taken my regular spot on the couch, laptop open, full of possibilities: poetry? Prose? Photo edits? Netflix?

"Let's paint the apartment!"

"…"

"I'm serious!" he asserted.

"Ha Ha Ha" I returned to staring at my laptop screen, trying to convince myself I had a busy day ahead.

"Seriously! Why not! Yes. We will paint the apartment. What colors?"

"Blues? A dark blue and a light." I figured I could humor him.

"Yes, blue is good. But we have too much blue already! The bookshelf is blue! The TV stand is blue!"

We spent the whole weekend painting the apartment: we settled on greens for the outdoors we so missed. The hours went by in giggles and How I Met Your Mother reruns. When He was focused on taping corners, I grabbed his cheeks leaving light green streaks across his face. He started chasing me about the apartment, as I jumped over our furniture, pushed haphazardly away from the walls. I fell onto the tarped-bed, and He jumped on top of me, grabbing by waist, leaving dark green handprints on my T-shirt. We rolled through paint and tarp, grabbing, kissing and nibbling every part of the other.

With paint globs in his eyebrows, I looked at him and thought how lucky we were to be quarantined together. I felt invincible.

"You know, when we come out of this COVID quarantine, we can face anything."

He rolled me over and kissed into a bliss; the newly green walls turning our love into a forest escape.

My phone reminded me of my return ticket from Uganda to DC; our medical mission trip had been canceled over a month ago, well before quarantine set in. It was Palm Sunday, but no churches would be gathering live. Sophia sent me a livestream from her favorite priest in Baltimore.

An ode to my faith of old.

On this emptied Palm Sunday
An image of vacancy
Warms these broken pieces of me,

My youthful faith gave me a story that fit what I felt:
An answer to my longing for more
A beat to the mundane, earthly slumber

She gave me a set, a system, a book
A foundation to learn from
And in her virtue, I found meaning.

But the equality she spoke of, I learned from a classroom,
Feminism and faith didn't quite reconcile.

The freedom she preached I learned from the queers:
To dance, to love, to be as God made us.

The Grace she preached, I learned from the messy world, and the steadiness of my
breath.

As time passed,
My life suddenly looked
Not like Faith wanted it

The questions kept crashing.
I held to this Faith until the stories which built me,
Finally tore me apart.

Knelt on a church pew
In a cathedral of old,
There came the gentle whisper I longed for:

"Give up these walls, for I am not here; I am in you."

Eddie called me; he was in the thick of yet another breakup with he-who-must-not-be-named. I could hear the quiver in his voice, as he outlined yet another argument they had, with all the old wounds resurfaced: the cheating, the lying, the lovemaking, the manipulating. Having lived with Eddie for three years, I could picture him perfectly. He would be sitting in his bed, fetal position, staring blankly out the window for the coming hours. He needed another body walking around, just to remind him that his heart, too, could continue to beat despite the echoing, emptying, pitfalling feeling of love lost once again. He needed to be fed and watered. He needed his apartment purged of all signs of he-who-must-not-be-named. But this was a quarantine. Eddie worked in the hospital. I shouldn't go over. I couldn't go over.

HEARTBREAK SURVIVAL GUIDE

The processing is painful, but it keeps your heart open and free. Don't callous over your pain.

Chose yourself. You are the miracle. You have grown, love this new you you've found yourself with.

The echoing, emptying, less than full feeling will overwhelm you. Again, and again. But slowly that echo will diminish.

Choose yourself. Don't call him. Don't text him. Delete his number. Take off his bracelet. This is choosing yourself.

Be still. Let the feeling overwhelm you. Be quiet. Write. Write letters. Write letters to him. To God. To you. These letters are part of your process. They're for you. Work. Wake up and keep going to work. Your work will bring you alive again.

Reach out. Even when you feel like a ghost at happy hour, be with your people. They will bring you alive again. Find a therapist. You can have Jesus and have friends and have a therapist too. Call your mother. She always breaks with you.

And slowly life will resume, and you'll laugh the deep laugh that you miss. And you'll feel whole again, and you'll never forget what he meant to you, how he changed you. And you'll learn that you are worthy. You will return to yourself. You will find peace. You will be able to sit with yourself again. All that you were and all that you will be you hold within yourself now.

And maybe someday, you'll see him across the bar, and you'll send him his favorite drink, and you'll raise your glasses to the yous that you were.

Why are you the way you are?
He asked with a smirk.
I love that He thinks of me.

WHY are you the way you are?
He said through gritted teeth.
A small annoyance.

Why are you the way you are…!
He chuckled with a smile,
A soft kiss.

When He glared, and didn't ask
I heard his screaming thought:
Why are you the way you are?

April 7th, 2020
The full moon is inside my house.

She's rising along my wide-open window
She sits on a building
Where she's not supposed to be.
my neighbor, the
city passer-byes pay her no mind

She ought to be a long reflection
upon a wayward sea
A blue that melts her longing
Across wide open waters

She ought to be shimmering
Behind shaking leaves
A forest light
For the trees encircling, overgrown

Instead she sits here with me
In this city unknowing
Hung like an echo,
illusive, longing

Recklessly, she spills
Even in this city
Over apartment buildings
Largely ignored.

Together
She's sitting with me, still.
Waiting like an echo
Of a nature long since lost. Remembered.

Irritated, *slightly*
I didn't want to walk, you see
But He did.
A small sacrifice to make for a partner,
But why can't he walk Himself, I do.
Irritated at myself for being irritated.

Laying on the floor,
Shavasana.
The floor feels heavy beneath me.
The floor pushes me forward
As my muscles spasm and
Finally letting go, melt.

My eyes open
To an orange hazy spot
Just right of midline
On the white ceiling.
It's not really there.

A heavy, redundant piano plays in the distance
Do I know this melody? It's not really there.
The melody comes from me, my piano plays on.
And suddenly I'm dancing,
Dancing over piano keys, redundant, heavy.
A smile breaks over me.

Dreamer; creator.
I BANG on the drums. BANG. BANG.
Now, I'm dancing through the tall grass.
As the melody carries me
An Irish dancer from somewhere joins me
We dance together, freely, shouting.

Have I totally lost it already? Am I seeing and hearing things? Are these hallucinations?
No, those who are psychotic don't question the psychosis.

Can I save him? I thought of Eddie and his slow heartbreak. I thought of how I wasn't there for him, how I couldn't be but should've been. I heard his voice in my own head, answering my questions of him.

Does he need saving? He retorted quickly.
You tell me...
His eyes turned outward, transfixed
by how the world out there
keeps moving when he can't.
I presumed.

Does he need saving?

Maybe my narrative is wrong.
maybe I'm too close-minded.
No.
He's become a thing
I don't recognize.
Lost in the world of Star-Crossed and Love Lost.

How do I remind him?

Of the man he once was, the
man he IS!
Replace his phone case. Replace his bracelet.
Replace every memory left by him, *manipulator*,
on the man I once knew,
my friend.

Was it ever Love?

He's gone because that's what he wants.
This is the new normal.
Love does not dishonor,
Love is not self-seeking.
Love rejoices in Truth.
But he's chosen this broken Love.

What then is True?

That we all need saving,
perhaps.
That the Love was broken, not him, my friend.

That we are each our own disaster,
perhaps our own miracle,
that we are our own to save.

Daydreaming:
Do you believe in magic?
Of course, I do,
haven't you felt it
it's all around.

My throne remains
stainless and glistening
on a sea-cliff palace
in a land I once knew:
Cair Paravel.

All but ruined,
fallen stone down the cliffside
I walk along the beach below
diving decidedly
into each crashing wave.

Like the endless sea,
my mind becomes a murky expanse
where all are welcome:
Slow grown coral, creatures of the deep,
and the sweet secrets carried in currents past.

Coming up for air,
as one must.
The twinkling of magic still tickles my toes.
I see the palace ruin: the magic of youth
a long-forgotten memory.

Yet there remain moments
of magic and spark
which rush over me like the waves.
And the ruined palace that is no longer
what it was,
becomes a foundation
of what it could be.

April 9th, 2020

16,780,000 claims for unemployment were filed in the past three weeks in the
United States.

This poem wants
to breath the
fresh spring wind,
full of sweet blooming scent.

This poem wants
to swim, recklessly
in the wide-open waters
of things unknown.

This poem wants for
nothing more than
to feel it's
beating heart
alive in this broken world.

Thinking of my far-off palace,
I am the castle ruin.
Pillars wrapped
in green choking ivy.

Pillars of white
standing like a beacon
others the lasting skeleton
a ruin, long since weakened.
Standing tall
like the Virtues they hold
standing strong,
though time may chip its elegance.

They whisper their words
through their cracks, a façade,
lost and transformed.
Empty, ruined, without weight to carry.

Someone on my Facebook feed posted a graph with percentages of cotton mask protection from pollen, pollution, bacteria, and viruses. Virus was at less than 5% protection. I didn't source or fact check. It only confirmed what I had thought: *we are grasping for answers in the dark and pushing solutions not based in evidence or science.* I looked over to the key hook where our home-made masks hung, wondering how anyone could think a scrap of cotton could save anything.

I researched the mask issue, recalling the new CDC guidelines suggesting everyone where masks in public places. Looking through the scientific literature, I found two articles which directly addressed efficacy of wearing masks with viral spread. In a sample study, those who wore surgical grade masks versus those who did not wear masks were found to have no difference in rates of infection for the SARS virus, suggesting that while wearing surgical masks post no harm, they are not effective in reducing viral transmission. Another study showed that those wearing home-made fabric masks actually had higher rates of viral transmission with influenza, suggesting home-made masks are actually deleterious.

That morning, we left our masks at home and walked to Target. We walked north on 14th street, passing the recently gentrified stores, some of which had boarded up in fear of looters. The stores that remained open—CVS, liquor stores, Trader Joe's —had six feet demarcations for customers to line up outside. Few people walked about with their masks snug over their noses and mouths. Most made a point to maintain the defined six feet radius around them, allowing others to pass in the opposite direction or changing their speed to accommodate their COVID space. As we traveled north, past U street and into Columbia Heights, a historically Latinx community, the street traffic increased greatly, with the majority of pedestrians without masks and paying no mind to social distancing rules. *Quarantine and distance really are a privilege*, I thought. Kids biked recklessly through the streets, hollering and popping wheelies. Schools had been canceled as to ensure shelter-in-place orders, to which these kids were clearly paying no mind. The whole neighborhood seemed bereft to the state of emergency which had swept the rest of the city.

As we approached the double doors, a security employer waved us away. Through his muffled mask, he stated we can only enter with face coverings, as ordered by the DC mayor as of
yesterday.

Another policy based on hearsay. I had made a point to check the DC governor's page regularly, to stay abreast of such policy changes. With media and news sources constantly writing about COVID progression and changes in governmental policies, it had become hard to separate suggested guidelines from governmental ordinances, which had become so specific to each state and even city. Terms circulated: Shelter-in-Place, State of Emergency, Lock Down, Curfew! With all the noise and news being pushed across multiple media sources, the primary government ordinances which outlined the actional definitions of each term were hard to find; it was difficult to ascertain how we were supposed to respond each day to the evolving crisis.

The convoluted news didn't matter at that moment. What mattered was this security officer was not letting us enter Target. My partner and I looked at eachother, each scanning the other for quick ideas.

"I left the masks at home...I'm sorry. You know how I read they are pretty much useless!"

"Ya, I didn't think to bring them either."

We took off our jackets—we had both worn light puffers that morning—and tied them around our necks, struggling to get the sleeves to cover nose and mouth without falling. Security let us through, apologizing for the inconvenience.

Target was nearly desolate, with masked employees walking through and restocking. We fidgeted with our makeshift jacket masks, the sleeves continuously sliding off our steep noses. My breath became hot and sticky, reverberating off the plasticky fabric. I started to overheat, readjusting the sleeves yet again, feeling claustrophobic.

"The degree of face touching is DEFINITELY outweighing any possible benefit of this"

My partner, noticeably annoyed, didn't even respond. We ditched the grocery list, grabbing the few essentials and left just to breath the open air. The shuffling pedestrians, the screaming kids on their bikes, the street vendors, all hit me by surprise; outside the apocalyptic Target, life was on seemingly unaware of the invisible perpetrator who, just one mile south, was wreaking panic and fear in every little whyte apartment.

Doubt. DOUBT!!
A curiosity: questions led to questions
Which brought me closer
To myself. Closer to God.

The doubt which built doubt
was answer in itself
Ever yearning for more
Proof that I was more.

Made for more.
Made for meaning. Pockets of air filled with
The feeling that more might
Be what truly exists.

Question to question
Finally, the foundation:
Was I wrong in my entirety?
Did we make it all up?

Were those sacred spaces
All but empty grasps
To lull my finality
Into the false framework of Meaning.

This Doubt-the doubt of all doubts
I stifled; feared to look into
And I carried her, unknowing
Like heavy stones, from place to place

But the weight did not belong to Doubt
But for the stifled, shame-filled Ego:
A fear that I might have been wrong
The testimony I professed, my identity, WRONG.

There is no Ego but the One
The mind but a mirror to some infinite Self
Headspace competes
Bought by the lies we tell ourselves:

That we must arrive
Arrive at the answers: wisdom. Well-adjusted.
That there is shame in confusion,

Shame in changing course.

Lies like to sit in the darkest corners
Deep sulci of the brain,
Light, breath, seeing breaks their shame,
Open, free.

There is no Ego but the Self
Yearning returns the mind to itself,
Practice cleanses the mirror to better reflect the Self
And meaning, as for meaning, I still have no answer.

April 11, 2020

The U.S. reported 518,892 cases and 20,109 deaths. Spain reported 161,852 cases and 16,353 deaths. Italy reported 152,271 cases and 19,468 deaths. Germany reported 117,658 cases and 2,544 deaths. France reported 93,790 cases and 3,339 deaths. China reported 84,218 cases and 3,339 deaths.

In the after:

If after ever comes:
We'll return to
the ease of
loving eachother in health.

Lest we remember how
sickness left us:
Straining for bridges
to cross the harrowing echo.

Yes, life goes on,
to easy nights
and laughter:
Friends, drink, folly.

But we will always know
what life's distractions cover:
With what we are left
when we are bare.

Easter.

Circling, climbing, mounting Doubt. Question of questions lead to more questions: the foundation, the assumption, the cliché, to fit in the box, my edge. Yearning; yearning for more, yearning for sacred explanations, to make sense of what has been done. The yearning is answer itself.

This Easter Sunday is quiet, a whisper. Empty without performance, without 1000 baptisms, the lights, the loudspeaker, the dresses and French braids. In the empty echo, God whispers. But God has always preferred the whisper, the empty church, the barren, the lost, even the questioning. At
least in my experience. God whispers within each of us.

And what of this crucifixion? An empty grave some 2000 years ago. The empty grave: fact or fiction. The empty grave says this world is not the last word. But what if it is? The empty grave says the sacred spaces for which you yearn is the ever after, the Truth. That yearning is answer itself. But what if it isn't? The empty grave says God is in you and God is in me. But what if we are just human, struggling, loving, laughing in these frail failing bodies.

Christ is risen! There is new life to be had, freedoms to be given. The questions seem just as everlasting as Christ is in you and Christ is in me; both became a promise that's never failing. Even in the cry of night, God whispers. Even though there is, always will be, a cry of the night, God whispers.

My brother's birthday. I sent him a planter and seeds, assuming he could use the project and it would fit on his tiny San Francisco apartment balcony. Two thousand miles felt like a lifetime away.

I woke up with a vague tingling feeling in my arm, along the lateral line from my elbow to my pinky was numb-ish. My neck was stiff. *Cervical radiculopathy? Saturday night palsy? Somatic ramifications of internal stress?*

In the evening we surprised my brother with a group Zoom call of family and friends. It was sheer chaos with every other tiny screen speaking over the other. It took my parents 30 minutes to login and figure out the camera and audio. *I should have walked them through this earlier in the afternoon!* One cousin shouted *Las Mañanitas* drunkenly as my mother shook maracas into the camera. Another cousin repeatedly cheers-ed the camera each time he refilled his tequila.

Things that create the Appearance of Deep Emotion
After Sei Shōnagon
Platitudes: Morality, Virtues, like
Philosophy, like Plato and his Forms,
Capital letters, like capital L-Love
or capital T-Truth.
Platitudes:
Well-crafted words,
whispered voices, secrets carefully retold.
Empty beautiful prose,
so full of beauty that it's
no longer empty.
Prolonged eye-contact,
fleeting eye-contact,
Drawn-out silences.
Fate, false destiny, coincidence,
Talk of Time continuums and Existence,
Questions, Wonder,
effortlessly placed Touch,
heartbeats racing, racing together
Dreams, loosely given
Banality dressed in silk: Platitudes.

The Light! The Light, she said!
A moment gripped her sweet soul:
Magical, like some heartstring melody
Neurons sparked, struck just, beauty:
Transcendental to behold.

But how to capture this Light
How to capture this feeling,
The magic. Impulse. Capture.
BLOCK, freeze.
It's the angle, she said!

Stop, a whisper.
Be still, a breath. She ignored.

SHOOT. Catch the twinkle. Yes!
The shot, click. Future deserves
To hold this moment in time.
To capture the Light. Behold:
Now annulled of its Beauty
Filled by glory of Captured and Clicked: a Sensation

It's not the thing that happened
or didn't happen.
It's the Not Being Heard.
The Pride and justification of the Thing,
which now has become a capital T-Thing
though really it was never about the thing.
Then it's the Not Being Heard
About Not Being Heard.
And so, it goes on.

I continued to notice the vague paresthesias in my arm, the sensation of pins and needles popping up in different parts of my arm a few times each day. My opposite wrist became painful at times, shooting pain when I put weight on it during my yoga practice. Having received and treated to remission a tenosynovitis of the wrist last year, I knew the best treatment was a high dose Ibuprofen taper, but with the news from France regarding higher complications in young patients on anti-inflammatory medications such as ibuprofen, I decided to stop most of my yoga practice. Without daily stretching, my neck felt tighter. The paresthesias continued.

Is this all psychosomatic? Am I so bored that I can suddenly feel body aches I used to ignore?

For Love

Give me a thousand kisses, the slow ones
that quiver, and I'll give you a thousand more.
Give me the old scotch in an ice-cold glass,
the one with dragon breath and a hint
of sweet honey in the back of my throat.
Give me a brown grass love, a barely make it
to the top of the hill love, but we'll keep climbing.
Huffing, puffing, and climbing.
Give me a heartbeat racing kind of love,
a tangled, messy, you said this, but baby I'm sorry
worth waking up at 3am,
a why can't you understand me,
snuggle me to death kind of love.
Bleach the tub and draw me a bath with
the dried rose petals from our last bouquet.
I want a love that feels like the whole wide world
like the crashing ocean,
wide, open, and raw with its currents that pull you
under, swept off your feet when you least expect it
kind of love. Give me three greasy Taco Bell chalupas
on day 49 (or is it 31?) of The Eschatological Isolation.
Give me a what I needed all along but never knew
kind of love: of free-falling, ever evolving,
everything is relative, and thus, nothing at all,
except for our love, kind of love.
Give me flowers in my cocktail, a tall American Beauty,
Foie gras to spit out, and green forest walls.
Rent me a red dress, and tell me how much more you'll
love me in five years, with crow's feet eyes.
Scoff at my music, scoff at my taste, scoff at my upspeak,
because I know you'd never live without it. But above
everything else, give me a love that believes.
Believes that we'll make it to the top of this mountain,
dance at the top of this mountain, in the sun-burnt
brown wind-blown grass, love

Midnight.
Words blur into stars, galaxies.
I wake with words
still on my tongue.

Tasting like mercury,
confused, lulled in a stardust sky.
The morning bird sings
shut up. I roll over,
onto wrinkled, lost words.
Scribble them into memory
onto the sulci of awareness!
Dear God, don't let me forget
*these sultry word*s

Light escapes, awakening
my dreams:
It was all a fantasy
of my midnight poem.

Write late into the night
and early with the songbirds
where words spill into fantasy
a poem of dreams rewrite reality.

Americans have started protesting the quarantine.

"People are the worst, aren't they?" I said as much to the room as to Him, who was at his desk with the Look of Concentration.

"I've said that from the beginning!" he replied, not changing the Look.

I've never felt such little sympathy for people, ever. Just stay fucking home. Protesters, PROTESTERS? This is not about freedom, or lack thereof. It is about respect for others, respect for safety of others, concern for the health of the nation. WHAT THE FCK do people not understand about a CRISIS.

My left arm tingled. My right wrist ached. My neck felt tight.

Studies started show pulmonary microemboli, or tiny blood clots in the lungs, being a possible complication of coronavirus. Maybe that's why patients being intubated didn't improve even after the virus cleared. Maybe that explained the total whiteout where lung was supposed to be seen on chest x-rays. Maybe that's why patients who were intubated weren't able to be extubated, weren't able to breath on their own after weeks of treatment. Studies out of New York and New Jersey started reporting over 95% mortality rate for patients who were intubated.

Black and Latinx Americans are dying at disproportionally higher rates as compared to white Americans from COVID-19.

Brown bodies,
My bodies,
Forgotten again. Forgotten,
     Of course.

It's the hypertension. The underlying diabetes.
     They said.
As though an explanation
     Could excuse the reality of numbers,
     Of injustice.

Of bodies left, uncared for, unnoticed.
Black bodies, brown bodies,
     Mi familia:
     The Within and The Without.

Left to the mercy
     Of our New Aged Parasite.
The new aged gunshot.
The new aged noose.

They said it would be The Great Equalizer.
No! No America, there is no Equalizer here!
There never has been.
This New Aged Parasite is but a mirror.

Then they ask, *who's*
     The Parasite looking back at me?
Where has he been hiding
     All this time?

Perhaps, hidden within
     The hypertension, the diabetes
     We labeled noncompliance.
Labeled miseducation, cultural difference.

Blamed these brown bodies.
No, America. There is no Equalizer here.
There never has been.
Look in the mirror, see
     The Parasite who stares
Blankley back, ravenous.

April 19th, 2020:

The United States recorded 746,332 cases with 35,676 deaths.
Spain reported 195,944 cases with 20,453 deaths.
Italy reported 178,972 cases with 23,660 deaths
Germany reported 139,897 cases with 4,294 deaths. *How are the Germans staying alive?*
The United Kingdom reported 120,067 cases and 16,060 deaths.
France reported 112,606 cases with 19,718 deaths.
China reported 88,405 cases, with 6,632 deaths. *Sure.*
Turkey reported 86,306 cases with 2,017 deaths.
Iran reported 82,211 cases with 5,118 deaths.
Russia reported 42,853 cases with 361 deaths.

I walked past a USPS womxn delivering the mail.

"GOD BLESS YOU MA'AM. THANK YOU."

She didn't respond. She was on a phone call, headphones in.

We fought about the nightstand. It was stupid.

We fought about the spilling water. It was stupid.

We fought about fighting too much. *That* was revelatory, even though we've had that fight ten times over. Because I want to talk through every last thing and he wants the conversation to be over.

Denial is breading grounds for poor communication and emotional suppression.

Over-thinking is breading grounds for false accusations and insecurities.

I woke up sad about all the fighting. He got up, and started getting ready for work, his 10AM all-staff meeting approaching. I didn't want to talk about it; we had said everything that needed to be said. I just wanted to stay in bed a few more hours. Maybe I'd read my kindle a while. He returns and asked what's wrong.

Slowly, I looked up at Him from the bed.

"Are you still sad about yesterday?"

"Yea..." My voice trailed. I knew we had logically resolved the argument; I didn't have anything else to say.

We fought about my morning depression. I deserve the space to feel what I feel. I should not have to live by the expectations of what He wants me to feel. I can't live with his desire to never feel sad or bad or sulky or tired or lazy or apathetic.

"But think about how *your* feelings make me feel! Think about where *your* way of *lingering in your feelings* has gotten us. You're so stubborn! I keep trying to make you feel better, but you don't want to."

The guilt trip; the I'm Selfish for giving myself space to feel. "I wish you wouldn't take my feelings so personally. I wish you would just give me space to process, and I will feel back to normal by noon."

"*Great*! We will just go on existing on your emotional schedule and see where that gets us without changing anything, like idiots on repeat."

On repeat. Life seemed to be on repeat.

He was right, I am stubborn. But I was right too, about his imposing expectations. If being depressed on the couch makes him feel like we've compromised, I'll sit on the couch instead of the bed.

That night we fought for hours.
Fought in circles
in *how did we get there* and *will this ever change*?
Floating in a nightmarish, hellish, blur.
Trapped.
Where will we find resolve?
I fought to remember the *before,*
to remember the I love you.
But I love you
I LOVE YOU,
I know

It comes in waves:
the fear of not being enough
the thought of having to start over
with someone new
who will not caress the rough parts of me
softly like you do.

It comes in waves
the not holding you
the loss of our future
our make-believe kids
our forest green apartment
the me I saw in your future.

It comes in waves
the thought of ending
as though one crack
makes the breaking inevitable.
Inevitable like the crashing waves
ceaselessly crashing.

It comes in waves
the fear of losing my Love.
When I least expect it fear drowns
out the memories of discovery and lust
of our easy Love before the waves came
as they come

In Case of Emergency

In case of emergency
be still.
Pull the blinds,
windows wide open to let
the day in.
Play Debussy and
reruns of Seinfeld.
Foam the milk with Kahlúa.
Lay down expectation,
thrown off armor at the ceasefire.
Be still and know that this too
will pass, clouds clearing
at the storm's end.
In case of emergency love quietly.
In case of emergency shower,
brush your damn teeth, and
wake.
Live slowly at first,
but soon, all at once.

Wednesday April 22nd, 2020

United States reported 822,239 cases and 41,683 deaths.
Spain reported 208,389 cases and 21,717 deaths.
Italy reported 187,327 cases and 25,085 deaths.
Germany reported 145,694 cases and 4,879 deaths.
United Kingdom reported 133,495 cases and 18,100 deaths.

Reality is but a reflection of our mind. I said it was a sigh, He said it was a scream. I said it was just one morning, one morning every few months that I was depressed, He said it had been daily, for weeks. He felt I don't give enough, that He gives more. I feel like I accommodate on every corner, and that He did not listen, did not *hear*, did not consider my experience to be just as legitimate as his own.

When we started to do the math and started the Tally of what I've given and what he has given, I know we have crossed some invisible line from which it is hard to recover. *I don't care about the Tally!* I care about making you feel loved and cared for, that I believe we can be more and better, that you believe I can be more and better. But how do we foster such feelings without regressing to the Tally of what I have done versus what you have done?

I started growing pimples. One for every fight. I remembered the little French Madeline and Miss Clavel, who woke with a fright in the middle of the night saying something is not right!! Each of my pimples were a little French Madeline screaming at me, *something is not right!*

I went on a long walk with Eddie; we hadn't seen eachother in weeks. We walked through winding streets of million-dollar homes on Kalorama Street, daydreaming of which we could buy together in some future where we made more than our below-minimum wage hourly salary and had paid off our growing $200,000 loans.

"I'd love to be quarantined with a backyard tennis court too."

"We have apartments; no matter how small we can't complain."

"I should stop complaining about the lines at Trader Joes..."

Thursday April 23rd, 2020

U.S. 861,394 cases; 44,152 deaths
Spain 231,024 cases; 22,157 deaths
Italy 189,971 cases; 25,549 deaths

Habibti, amor, ammura, my love:

The days feel inconsequential,
I know. And,
I know that you know
there is much to be done:
love, write, read, learn. And,
I know that you know
that every moment matters,
though the days slip endlessly
to eternity. Remember
the lotus who floats on the Nile.
Remember how she reaches
above her muddy waters,
ripe with the tension
of birth and rebirth. Every night
she sinks into deep crystal blue.
Every morning she blossoms,
Above her muddy waters.

You are the moon
with endless phases
to grow through.

You are the lotus flower,
who rises with the sun
above her muddy waters.

Friday April 24th, 2020

U.S. 891,957 / 45,757
Spain 219,764 / 22,524
Italy 192,994 / 25,969
Germany 150,383 / 5,321
U.K. 143,464 / 19,506
France 122,577 / 22,245
Turkey 104,912 / 2,600
China 88,653 / 4,632
Iran 88,194 / 5,574
Russia 68,622 / 615
Brazil 52,995 / 3,670
Belgium 44,293 / 6,679
Canada 42,750 / 2,197
Netherlands 36,535 / 4,289
Switzerland 28,677 / 1,309
India 23,452 / 723

Do you have the Antibodies?
        Tested.
Did you brave the new-aged dragon?
Covid-light. *Maybe?*
Who can be tested? *Me, surely?*

Do you hold secret sword and shield,
        Well within your blood,
        Forward marching with each heartbeat?
Status: passed, braved, positive
        Antibodies.

Do you wear the new
        Signet ring, a cure for only you?
Your pass for freedom.
Do we pin a scarlet letter upon your breast?
Marked, superior, free, survivor, able.

Does your Antibody cry,
        Tears of silent anguish screaming for those fallen?
A mounting toll: bodies, lives
Upon which you stand, your Antibody.
Elevated above the rest.
        Separated from the Dead, the Dying, the Sick, the Stuck, the Quarantined.

Does your Antibody protest,
        Marching for false freedoms?
Without safety in sight,
With righteous anger and pride,
        Marching into the unknown, brazen
        Against Science, against Law, against Neighbor, against kindness.

Are you our savior?
The Antibody, the cure in blood:
        Replicated, transmitted, shared.
Why does *my* Antibody,
        Robust, strong, survived, breathed,
        Mock *his* Antibody, unmounted, left for loss of breath, Antibody but clots in
his lungs?

Is your pass to freedom,
        A pass to serve?
To stand up front, your shield for all. Your Antibody for all.

All humanity's hope
       Found by a bloody, sick-stained, death-tolled Antibody.
But who will be tested? *Me, surely?*

We rented a car; wiped it clean with Clorox. There were no cars on the roads as we left DC.

"Screw the virus; I'll keep this COVID traffic."

We drove with the windows down to circulate the stale air; the fresh air whipped through our unkept, overgrown hair. The empty road ahead restored the feeling of freedom to our mildew-covered minds. Shenandoah valley: hillscape views, dollhouse Victorians with delicate trim, barns glimmering with fresh red coat. Cows grazed happily, unaware of the stifled isolation set before humanity. But with every picturesque view was that of abandonment: old houses overrun with ivy, rotting barns, trailer parks with tattered American flags. We passed a confederate flag, strung high above a light-green Victorian with a white picket fence. The sign ahead read *Historic Downtown.*

"Every small town thinks their downtown his *historic.*"

Confederate flag in rear view, I thought, "Let's find a creamery; possibly the only good thing about old-town America."

"It will be closed. Everything is closed. The world is closed! The WORLD is closed!" He repeated.

"I don't know that the *world* is closed. The trees, the trails, the world is wide open!"

"CIVILIZATION! CIVILIZATION HAS CLOSED."

"Yes. Yes, it has."
I wondered if the cows noticed us zipping by, us city-dwellers, foreigners, seeking the fresh mountains like a salve for our sunken hearts. I told my long-winded stories of past memories as my partner drove on, weaving through empty lanes and flipped through his old playlists.

Many songs later, we pulled onto a grassy, pebbled road, drove under a wrought-iron train-tracked bridge, and onto the cool sun-kissed banks of a slow-dancing river. We jumped out of the car and He immediately shouted song lyrics. The tree branches shuffled, the breeze through the leaves like a response to our disruption. We walked a trail along the riverbank, singing. I skipped, and laughed, and twirled, with the echo of my lover's shouts still widening my smile. I turned around abruptly and flung my arms around his neck and let my chest push into his. Looking doe-eyed over our long, brown noses, I whispered "I feel like your heartbeat."

His arms around my waist, he picked me up and spun me in circles then quickly nibbled my nose and chin and eyebrows and ears, "I feel like silliness!" he smirked with a sparkle in his eye, then in a whisper, "I love your eyes. They are bright and brown, but a special brown, like they catch the light when you look at me."

I felt warm and tingly, which made me realize I hadn't felt truly, deeply, recklessly loved in weeks. We'd been on edge, at each other's every annoying gesture with the apartment walls closing in, but we were finally free. I smiled; he is colorblind, you see. "My brown eyes are light because they have green, which you may never see." The wandering trail surprisingly led us back to the rental car; we switched spots as I took the driver's seat.

We were free; finally, free to be silly and loud and loving. With a new scenery came our old love, a love that was easy. Our silences were no longer pregnant of my over analysis or relationship anxiety. The replayed arguments finally stopped. The *I wish I'd just said this but don't want to bring it up again* melted away because finally our love of the other refocused into view, and a spectacular view it was. I looked at him, the silhouette of his profile, the patch of his scruff he missed at last shave, which was now longer than the rest, and smiled that silly maybe a lunatic but no one is watching smile, remembering that this love wakens my slumber, that here sitting in this car is the most precious thing I've ever held.

On the drive home, we fought about my driving.

"You're so absent minded! You're *always* absent minded! I WISH you'd be more perceptive; it would change *everything!*" Suddenly the street sign I whizzed past, thus missing our turn, was a comment on my entire character.

My voice quivered. *How did we get here?* How did a wrong turn come to feel like He resents every part of my personality, like everything I do is wrong just because it is not how *He* would do things! I have no defense to his arguments, which felt like stab wounds. I felt open, raw, bleeding from the holes where he stabbed me then pulled out the knife. I couldn't bear being made to justify myself to my Love. My silence angered Him.

"Can you just SAY what is on your mind, what you are thinking! I hate having to guess."

He's right; arguments often shock me into silence, short-lived catatonia being my response to feeling overwhelmed, the words swirling so slowly while the feelings build quickly and I can barely find a sentence of substance to utter. But how could I explain how this small disagreement felt like *everything*; our incompatibilities highlighted to the point of hopelessness, irredeemable. The space between us grew to a chasm the longer I couldn't speak. How could some small error of mine remind Him of an entire aspect of my personality which frustrates Him so.

We pulled over and sat in the mess of what had become of our beautiful, happy, easy Love. A Love that had been present just moments before. Was our Love so tenuous, so fragile, so easily shattered?

"I wish you could be more patient, more kind towards my failures. I feel so attacked, like there is so much resentment between us when with one mistake, you challenge my very character."

I am not sure how we escaped the slippery argument which had surfaced time and again over the prior weeks: how we are simply so different. I wanted kindness and patience, and he wanted efficiency. He felt like I will never understand Him, but sounded like the teenager who, stuck in the egoism of their developing mind, are convinced there is no other human alive who can understand the nuance of their emotional experience. He thinks He understands me because He can articulate why I react emotionally and what I want, but He maintains his ways are better irrespective of the emotional toll taken on me. He thinks I am uncompromising in my ineptitude to function more like him, which is not untrue, but what He can't admit is He is just as uncompromising in his insistence that his way is Correct. Our two egos entangled and suffocating, crashed within the stillness of our car, tucked away in some Virginia backroad highway.

"Why are you this way!" He said with a forced chuckle, announcing our ceasefire. We switched seats, and I wiped my tears as He drove onward, through highways surrounded by a green tunnel of tangled trees much like the painted apartment towards which we barreled ever forward.

After dinner He made me a dirty martini. I had loved the last one. I played one of our songs loud and we danced naked in our socks, sliding through the apartment till I fell onto the carpet. He wrapped me in a blanket and pulled me around shouting DEAD BODY DEAD BODY as I laughed uncontrollably. He collapsed onto me and nibbled my shoulder.

"I could be a cannibal of there was no other option. Obviously, I wouldn't eat you."

"Psychopath." I couldn't stop laughing for an hour.

"She's buffering! She's broken!" He yelled to the walls as my laughter continued. Then He crawled over me, my body still wrapped like a burrito in the blue staticky blanket, and whispered, "Boo boo, did I break you?" I held my tongue for as long as I could, maybe seven seconds, then burst into more maniacal laughs. Nothing was particularly funny aside from our heightened silliness. We had months' worth of laughs to get out, a psychological outpouring of emotion, the small happinesses we'd failed to recognize over the past month for my general somnolence.

Quarantine

In the worst hour of the worst season
            of the worst year of a whole people
a man set out from the workhouse with his wife.
He was walking—they were both walking—north.

She was sick with famine fever and could not keep up.
            He lifted her and put her on his back.
He walked like that west and west and north.
Until at nightfall under freezing stars they arrived.

In the morning they were both found dead.
            Of cold. Of hunger. Of the toxins of a whole history.
But her feet were held against his breastbone.
The last heat of his flesh was his last gift to her.

Let no love poem ever come to this threshold.
            There is no place here for the inexact
praise of the easy graces and sensuality of the body.
There is only time for this merciless inventory:
Their death together in the winter of 1847.
            Also what they suffered. How they lived.
And what there is between a man and woman.
And in which darkness it can best be proved.

Eavan Boland, Dublin, Ireland
Published 2001; died April 27, 2020

If I don't make it,
Just know
[I love you]
I want to be
Buried on the moon.
[and I love you]

The candle wax melting, spilling over.

Rushing to class, spilt coffee burned fingers.

Laughing together over the fight cried through.

Not knowing the day. Not knowing the week. Cursing the whole of the year [of 2020].

Breaking up after the I Love You only to meet in different studio in a different city in a different body, and never letting go.

How time passes, I'll never know.

Time is but a construct, I'll always repeat.

Still, in small ways, the world tells us time is a Truth we can never outrun.

April 29th, 2020

Over one million cases recorded in the US. Over three million cases recorded worldwide.
MILLIONS like the moments that pass in silence between us,
like the cells in my eyeball.
Just 137 million cells defining my reality,
like millions of cosmic realities but we are found in just this one.
Millions, like the memories that flash before the I Love You and the million more from now until Death Do Us Part,
like the million watts of tension itching for freedom as I watch life through the window,
like the flaps of a butterfly in her short life.
Just one million?
One million, like the weight of anxiety to walk outside, to breath someone else's air, to be sick,
to be infected, to be defined as One Million.
One million lives written into history.
One million times an invisible threat caught hold.
One million in a nation who thought their strength was in millions.
One million unprepared, let down, failed.
The weight of millions like the fleeting hope caught in millionth breadth.

April 30th, 2020

U.S. 1,068,557 62,708
Spain 213,435 24,543
Italy 205,463 27,967
U.K. 171,253 26,771
German 159,119 6,288
France 129,581 24,376
Turkey 120,204 3,174
Russia 106,498 1,073
Iran 94,640 6,028
China 88,888 4,633
Brazil 85,380 5,901
Canada 85,380 3,082
Belgium 48,519 7,594
Netherlands 39,316 4,795
Peru 36,976 1,051
India 33,610 1,075

If I don't make it through,
Burry me on Mars.
I don't want to be with the failed human race forever.

May 1st, 2020

May you be kind, May you be warm
May you be salve for my sullen soul.
May you open my heart and keep it steady.
May the work of our tending
Finally grow

There are pieces
of myself I'd rather not see.
These broken stories
yearn to be heard, loved, redeemed.
But they quiver in the mirror,
fearful of the light.

Sometimes it feels like
I am all but shards of glass:
broken, bleeding at her edges,
searching to reflect
her undiscovered Truth.

Walking on glass, tip-toed
as to not shatter
my already broken pieces
scattered about the floor.

This floor, my foundation
the mirror, my truth, now
remnants of a slow collision
in pieces, but somehow free.

We fought again. I wanted to snuggle, to be close and tender. But he was tired. He let me give him a back massage, which I doubt he wanted. Who doesn't want a back massage? I gazed at him, without expectation, knowing he wanted to fall asleep, I just gazed. Love bubbling out my eyeballs—that look of overwhelming love: The Crazy Eyed Love. He asked me to stop. Four times. Finally, I yielded and stared at the ceiling, still bubbling over with the Crazy Eyed Love. He felt my Crazy Eyes, though no longer the object of my physical stare, and he got frustrated because he just wanted to sleep.

"I'm sorry for not respecting your space." But he was still frustrated; he went on about his frustration, of just wanting to sleep, of me not respecting his boundaries, which he stated.

I repeated, "I'm sorry I disrespected your space. Why are you still frustrated?"

He got up to pee. But he came back more frustrated. Finally, he realized my actions made him feel guilty. Like he didn't love me well. Like he didn't give me enough attention. Like he wasn't enough. Otherwise I would not be in bed longing and asking for more attention with the Crazy Love Eyes. Then he was frustrated that I didn't identify his guilt before he stated it, as though I was expected to know his emotions before he did. I told him to be more transparent with his emotions, just like he had asked of me.

It all seemed reasonable stated out step by step, emotion by emotion. But somehow in the midst of conflict, it felt like a hurricane closing in. Like an echoing, emptying, guttural spiral which pulled my insides and spit them out all over the green, putrid walls. Like I was right in the middle of Chaos, but it was hollow. Like a raging, thunder-filled storm which suddenly stops leaving nothing but drenched, sallow things in silence. Like a black hole of negative space, pulling gravity into itself, where things go to disappear. Like suddenly in the midst of it all, I forget what even we are fighting about, what we are fighting for, all I know is to Fight, Thrash, Flail Scream. Like there is stuff within me that I know years to Cry Out, but I am at a loss of words, not knowing what to cry about. Like my wordlessness is ammunition, proof that I, in fact, have nothing to cry about, leaving me like a girl crying wolf. But I trust the hairs that stand up on my neck telling me there is a wolf about this darkness, though my eyes and mind can't find it.

CIRCUMSTANCES: my emotions had become so circumstantial and so dependent on His. When He had a good day, I had a good day. When He had a busy workday, I became needy, insecure. I remembered words from Rumi, who said "Sufism is to feel Joy in the heart when Anguish comes."

Where did my internal Joy go? How did my emotional stability become dependent on another? Does that make me nothing but a Parasite, leaching?

Was this what they mean when they say Love is hard? The aching, treacherous building of a bridge across the raging waterfall that is this life in which we find ourselves? If this is Love, then hard doesn't begin to cover it. Is this a Love I want to fight for? Am willing to drown for?

The news had started to shift. What was anticipated to be a quarantine of weeks, months at worse, was beginning to look like a perpetual future. Experts were saying, THERE IS NO EVIDENCE TO BELIEVE COVID-19 WILL DOWNTREND BY THE HOT SUN OF SUMMER. There was no end in sight. The White House had proven completely incompetent, as universities, colleges, and governors planned for the future, each according to their own discretion. Cities and counties who had reopened their homes and marketplaces suffered new spikes in case numbers and deaths. Engineer and COVID-model maker Tomas Pueyo named the impeding future of coronavirus The Hammer and the Dance, naming strict national lockdowns the Hammer, and the attempts to reopen society the Dance, noting that each time a handful of people or places attempt normalcy, there will be an increase in case numbers, and thus a new normalcy-shattering, driving The Hammer of new restrictions. The Hammer and the Dance could go on for 18 months, for two years, until a vaccine is successful and well-trusted enough to take. All that scientists seem to know is the future is bleak, we may never return to society as we knew it. The new normal is the Unknown, and we must accept it.

The isolation started to feel like the end times. My life, my relationship, had succumbed to the Law of Entropy, that all things tend towards chaos. There were no answers, no certainties, and very little upon which to find footing.

All I began to know was of Love; this Love of building, plank by excruciating plank, a bridge and, no matter how guttural and painful the building may be, never doubting that He too is building his bridge, that somehow, somewhere, in some undefined future our bridges would meet in the middle, finally And as the poet Rumi says, I'll dance with Him there, cheek to cheek. The waters will continue to rage but we will be safe in the other's arms, on our wooden bridge, no railing, just hard-fought planks and rope whipping through the howling wind.

Awakened midnight,
by the sweet smile,
The all too familiar,
Burnt-white haze
Of the full faced moon.

The moon sits inside
My apartment window, again.
How she remembers
Every longing cry
Of my war
-torn heart

How she holds
My dreams and sorrows
With steadiness of glow,
I don't know.
All I know,

Is the sweet summer moon
Woke my gazing mind
At midnight.
My lover left,
Asleep in a daze.

She whispered her secret
Sweetly to me:
We all pass through phases
From empty to be full,
From empty to be free.

Chapter 2: The Reckoning

I thought I could write my own ending. I thought my writing could change my reality. I thought accepting the Unknown as reasonable and expected would heal the wounds I'd gathered because of it. I thought I'd open the blinds, turn off the radio, and find a version of myself within the quiet. A version of myself who was resolute and strong; strong enough to weather whatever came before her with grace. I thought I could write her into existence.

In the quite I found nothing but a shiver, as goosebumps crawled down my back.

I would be graduating medical school the end of this week. A dream I had held for a lifetime, one for which I had sacrificed my very sense of self. An accomplishment which had meant everything to my parents and family. And yet, I felt nothing.

May 13th, 2020

U.S. 1,397,416 cases 84,102 deaths
Russia 242,271 cases 2,212 deaths
U.K. 229,705 cases 33,186 deaths
Spain 228,691 cases 27,104 deaths
Italy 222,104 cases 31,106 deaths
Brazil 188,974 cases 13,149 deaths
Germany 171,306 cases 7,634 deaths
Turkey 143,114 cases 3,952 deaths
France 140,734 cases 27,074 deaths
Iran 112,725 cases 6,783 deaths
China 89,136 cases 4,633 deaths

Dear Medical School:

With much pride on my back,
I set out for a journey,
of healing humanity,
of *defining medicine.*

But quickly she became,
a shattering echo.
She weighted me down
with all that she took:
small pieces of me, chip by chip.

She smothered my nights,
many weekends she stole.
I started not to recognize
the puffy, morning eyes
staring back at me.

She followed me like a shadow,
pushed into the corners where I stood.
Cowering behind circles
of doctors I couldn't hear.

And slowly she fashioned
a passion in me.
Sweetly she strengthened
the hope of what I could be.

To my first patient, my White Coat glimmered,
his youthful body shattered by gunshots.
Wide-eyed and weary, his eyes woke
To my White Coat, no weathered and weathered.

By my White Coat,
many named me doctor,
But she was short, so I remembered,
No, that's not me.

With every tear and every victory,
she hung as the weight upon my shoulders.
With a breadth of healing, learning, and hope,
My White Coat insisted, doctor to be.

And that same short White Coat,
Who whispers memories

of having loved and lost some infinite self
healed the doubt which had grown in me.
The student who cowered, crippled, and shrugged
Became curious, confident, astute.
Welcoming my new White Coat as an old friend,
I learned to love the doctor who grew in sacrifice's stead.

I do solemnly swear by that which I hold most sacred:

That I will be loyal to the profession of medicine and just and generous to its members;

That I will lead my life and practice my art in uprightness and honor;

That into whatsoever house I shall enter,
it shall be for the good of the sick to the utmost of my power,
I, holding myself aloof from wrong, from corruption, from the tempting of others to vice;

That I will exercise my art solely for the care of patients,
and will give no drug, perform no operation for a criminal purpose,
even if solicited, far less suggest it;

That whatsoever I shall see or hear of the lives of people, which is not fitting to be spoken, I will keep inviolably secret.

These things I do promise in proportion as I am faithful to this oath
may my happiness and good repute be ever mine— the opposite if I shall be forsworn.

I recited my Oath of Hippocrates alongside many of the 20,000 graduating medical students across the country joined by spirit and internet.

We started packing. We would be leaving our beloved city of Washington DC to start my residency in Tampa, Florida. It felt like a lifetime away, but we would be driving South in a matter of weeks.

May 19th, 2020
U.S. 1,536,451 91,937
Russia 299,941 2,837
Brazil 271,628 17,971
U.K. 248,818 35,341
Spain 232,037 27,778

These four walls,
we painted ourselves
green like the blossoming,
living, thriving forest.

These four walls,
so sweetly did they plant us,
Long love lost in eachother
with memories held in each corner.

Even when the walls became
mirrors,
we learned to love the
monsters staring back at us.

And the walls which
found us, finally
demolished the walls
which deemed us.

The boxes stacked quickly,
high against our green walls.
Wistful mornings found us,
weary eyed between the sheets.

Slow brewed coffee hung
thick in the air like
the dreams we carried
from midnight til morn

I became a stack
of boxes: transient, stiff
filled with a lifetime of
memories shared without
knowing where to find
them.

Unsure, still hesitant and
fearful, in waiting:
waiting to be opened,
waiting to be embraced,
waiting to be welcomed home.

May 25th, 2020

U.S. 1,669,745 98,184
Brazil 374,898 23,473
Russia 353,427 3,633
U.K. 261,184 36,834
Spain 235,400 26,834

I prayed for challenge, wistfully
from my easy saunter.
I wanted challenge,
until he came knocking.
I said I wanted challenge,
until challenging was all we had become.

Still, the truth is, I chose
challenge day after day,
just to watch
my wings spread
and conquer

I never believed in
Goodbyes,
I believe in *I'll see
you soon.*

Eddie came over
and I couldn't say goodbye.
I had nothing to give.

But he,
He gave away
his favorite art piece:
an antique telecom
from a sunken submarine.

I remembered that
I fell in love with
His generous heart.

He had lost his parents,
and then he lost his car.
Then he lost his father's Rolex.
Then he lost his suitcase.
And somewhere along he must have learned:
we grow by letting go
and we live at the empty heart
of giving all that we've found

May 28th, 2020

U.S. 1,729,524 cases 101,611 dead people
Brazil 438,238 cases 26,754 dead people
Russia 379,051 cases 4,142 dead people
U.K. 269,127 cases 37,837 dead people
Spain 237,906 cases 27,119 dead people
Italy 231,732 cases 33,142 dead people
Germany 179,717 cases 8,411 dead people
Turkey 160,979 cases 4,461 dead people
India 158,333 cases 4,531 dead people
France 149,071 cases 28,662 dead people

May 31st, 2020

I was leaving a city I had come to call home, leaving for yet another foreign land on my journey to becoming a doctor. California born and bred, I was extremely reluctant to give my heart to the nation's capital, the city who had welcomed me as a medical student five years prior. And despite my West-Coast allegiance, I had come to love Washington DC—with her neoclassical pillared buildings alongside colorful brick row homes, all with Lady Justice sitting in our skyline to watching our every moment. Aside from the usual politics, protesting, and plethora of museums, I had come to fall I in love with what is collectively known as @theOtherDC—back alley neighborhoods, speak-easy bars, hidden gardens, and of course, the brightest, youngest, most diverse and welcoming citizens that made up the city.

My pride in DC had grown exponentially over the past few months during quarantine. My peers and colleagues not only welcomed every CDC guideline, but went out of their way to ensure the comfort and support of our community. My medical student colleagues had been volunteering in numerous ways, providing free testing across the city, providing day care for first-line workers, and feeding the kids who had relied on school meals. Mayor Bowser had maintained such strict and forward-thinking precautions regarding quarantine and mask wearing that the numbers reflected the dedication of our little city: our coronavirus cases were plateauing and remained amongst the lowest of all urban US cities. The District's reported data for Sunday, May 31, 2020 includes 56 new positive coronavirus cases, bringing the District's overall positive case total to 8,857, with deaths of two elderly citizens.

The last two days of my life in DC had been perfect; so perfect I thought I may have plucked Friday and Saturday out of an old gilded memory. Restaurants along 14th street had opened their doors, serving cocktails in containers to passersby. The residents of Dupont circle were wearing colorful masks, bootie shorts, and rainbow tanks tops as they rollerbladed, dog-walked, and longboarded down 16th street. I chatted with a group of drag queens in front of DIK (Dupont Italian Kitchen) bar, all maintaining 6 feet apart, as they shared the newest initiatives of their non-profit. With Pride month around the corner, and the harsh summer heat still at bay, there was an easy joy in the air as familiar and light as the cicadas' melody from the trees.

Sunday evening, I opened the windows of my Dupont studio apartment, to let the summer vibrance in. Not ready to say goodbye to the city in which my California heart had found an East Coast home, I sat on the ground and stared at the mountain of boxes: life as I had known it packed away. Movers would be here in the morning to help my frail arms carry these boxes into a moving van, which would drive 900 miles south.

A drizzly DC morning, we packed everything we owned into a U-Haul.
We drove down 17th street, through Dupont Circle,
Along the National Mall,

An onto the highway,
South.

Mid-afternoon, somewhere on the road in Virginia,
Just before North Caroline
I read the breaking news.
George Floyd was killed in Minneapolis, Minnesota
by police.

I had read about Ahmaud Arbery who was killed during a civilian's arrest
in February
in Georgia.

I had read about Breonna Taylor who was killed during a no-knock search warrant
by police in March
in Kentucky.

Another one.
George Floyd died May 29th, 2020, on that perfect DC day.
And we all knew the truth,
that he was murdered.

Demonstrators and protestors marched all over the country.
For Breonna Taylor,
For Ahmaud Arbery,
For George Floyd

I had pledged a solemn oath
to the care of patients,
with justice and generosity,
with uprightness and honor,
to the best of my ability.

How many oaths
go unbound,
bent, and broken
as black and brown bodies
are killed in the hospitals
by a virus we know not.

How many oaths
go unbound,
bent, and broken
as black and brown bodies
are killed in the streets
by lips which had uttered
such oaths as mine?

We continued our journey south
as the city we loved and left
became home to
freedom fighters
who refused to keep quiet.

We continued our journey
in our silence
as the world, erupting with
the sound of
silenced voices.

Driving through Savannah:

The country aches like
sallow, swinging Spanish moss
yearning for roots but
hanging from tree branches.

The country screams like the
eighteen-wheeler barreling down
its Southern highway, like
the bumpy roads hidden away by
the wilderness of trees;
its engine revving
just to keep pace.

The country's sorrow falls like
the summer storms: Hot rain drops smashing
the sizzling asphalt
demanding to be heard, and
the thunder shaking stale air,
demanding change.

The country blooms like
the wide-open magnolia flower
in the middle of the muggy forest,
grown by just enough sun which
breaks through the leaves of
her overgrown, neighboring trees.

She is a storm who says:
I built these roads with
ancestors' backs; I
tamed these forests for
your settled cities; I
am this country,
too.

Tallahassee:

The storm clouds lingered like
the inevitability of his loaded gun:
waiting for another one,
waiting for another one.

And when the storm
finally arrived,
my body rumbled like
the breaking thunder.

I opened the door to
the rushing wind,
"A storm is coming"
as I lingered in the doorway.

"It storms every day"
He stepped out, irreverently.
Unafraid to become the
free falling raindrops.

And when the rain came,
it poured down from blue skies
leaving me wonder,
from where her tears fell.

The storm which passed
watered her Earthy skin,
leaving her soaked and
ready for More. Expectant.

But also left her shattered like
her treasured talavera
pushed over by
the storm's wind.

But her flowers kept blooming
atop the soil
strewn across the
sweltering ground.

June 5th, 2020

U.S. 1,922,741 110,277
Brazil 672,846 35,930
Russia 467,073 5,851
U.K. 284,868 40,465
India 246,628 6,929

I read the news every day. The protestors marched onward; in Minneapolis, in DC, in Oakland, in Memphis, in Atlanta. I read James Baldwin, Amiri Baraka, Langston Hughes, and Maya Angelo. I found Black-owned businesses in my new town of Tampa. I learned about Daniel Prude, and before him Elijah McClain, and before him Miles Hall, and before him Joseph Dewayne Robinson. The work of learning was endless and heartbreaking; and just like the protestors I had to keep marching in my own ways.

I sat in my new empty apartment; the walls echoed a harrowing silence. I thought of myself days prior, sitting in my DC apartment and wondered if the world will ever return to carefree sense of normal. What even was normal, other than a blissful ignorance of the prejudges we carried? Unlike previous BLM protests in response to the murders of Trayvon Martin or Michael Brown, the outrage and fierce passion that spread across the country upheld a certain imminence, a righteous demand for change, and a sense that there was no going back to the before. It was a great reckoning and the emergence of a second pandemic—but this one did not strike suddenly one day from a tiny marketplace; this one had been hiding within our minds and hearts for centuries.

This new Florida I had just met continued in oblivion. There were no shouts in Tampa, Orlando, or Miami; no protesters to be found or joined. No masks were worn in the streets. Florida remained unaware of the state of the country and world. Florida cases were skyrocketing because its citizens did not head to the CDC quarantine precautions. It felt deeply disconcerting that the world I read and saw on the news was not the world around me. My new home state remained normal: unaware of the nations' cries. And normal looked like death.

It feels like
dragon's breath from my lungs;
like hot tears streaming;
like wanting to crush glass
in my hands
just to feel the gritty cuts
of my fingers;
like an emptying pit,
echoing the wordless
feeling in my gut.

June 10th, 2020

The United States reported 2 million cases of novel coronavirus with over one hundred thousand
deaths.

Aching for
how to
keep fighting.

Oluwatoyin Salau disappeared from Tallahassee, Florida on June 6th after tweeting details of a sexual assault by a man who had offered her rest in his home. She was confirmed dead on June 15th, 2020.

She should have known better.

She lived as though
the world she fought for
was the world we live in.

One where a man
could be of God,
whose hand could be trusted,
whose home could be restful.

Her resistance was to live in the world
that she believed in,
but the World Which Knew Better
ground her body to the dust.

June 17th, 2020

U.S. 2,170,258 117,680
Brazil 923,189 45,241
Russia 552,249 7,468
India 354,065 11,903
U.K. 299,683 42,153

And I feel my silence echo like
the empty apartment
whose walls yearned to
tell stores of every pealing
layer of our painted façade.

Like the eerie, sudden calm
just below the crashing
ocean waves: a semblance of
security amidst the tumult of
strong, silent undercurrents.

Like our far removed
new, Southern dwelling,
free form the sirens, the hustle,
the helicopters, the motorcades
of our beloved city's screeching story.

I was wrong. The old peer-reviewed scientific articles I had read the month prior had been disproved. It had become clear that countries and cities which upheld a mask mandate were shown to have decreased and significantly lower coronavirus case burden. The masks were slowing the spread. While DC upheld the mask mandate from early quarantine, even with new data, Florida did not follow suite. The president did not follow suite. Floridians continued frequenting their favorite restaurants and bars. I struggled to keep my distance from non-mask wearers at the grocery store who had no intention of remaining socially distant from strangers.

Recognizing it is exhausting to
live these days, to keep up with
the ever-changing narrative,
media, news, and knowledge.

Recognizing my exhaustion is but
the smallest fraction of
the daily, lived reality of
my Black hermanos.

Making space to
breath, to rest.
Recognizing my exhaustion is
no excuse to stop learning,
engaging, growing.

Dreary like
endless humidity
hanging, stifled
across the summer sky.

Lethargic from
sleepless nights,
tossing and nightmarish;
the dawn drudges unto day.
And hope,
that sweet fickle thing,
left me like the dew drops
dried in summer's heat.

So often
we see things by
their parts:
scattered pieces,
strewn across lifetime
and memory.

What hope we carry
for the sign of relief,
in finally
finding home with
the wholeness
of it all.

June 27th, 2020

U.S. 2,525,892 cases 125,521 deaths
Brazil 1,313,667 cases 57,070 deaths
Russia 626,779 cases 8,958 deaths
India 508,953 cases 15,685 deaths
U.K. 310,250 cases 43,514 deaths

Despite the darkness and
depths we've endured
The future, this world,
is ours I am assured.

Keep fighting, my dear.
Keep dancing, heart open.
We are in it together,
no matter the year,
no matter the force.
June 29th, 2020

They say big hearts
are for breaking,
but blessed is she who
dares take life in full:
only in fullness may we
feel our hearts awaking.

They say big hearts
are for breaking,
perhaps that's why
we find ourselves,
on this path,
always shaking.

Florida had become the epicenter of the second wave of the pandemic. The
daily death tolls of the state were making new records every day.

Chapter 3: Is this the beginning or the end?

July 1, 2020

It has been half a century since the civil rights movement, and since the Israeli occupation of the West Bank; 28 years since the LA Uprising; 8 years since Trayvon Martin was murdered; 6 years since Michael Brown was murdered; 313 days since the murder of Elijah McClain; 184 days since the virus was announced as a local outbreak; 165 days since the first sars-cov-2 case landed in the United States; 130 days since the murder of Ahmaud Arbery; 113 days since Mayor Bowser announced a state of emergency in the nation's capital; 111 days since the murder of Breonna Taylor; 107 days since I had been inside a hospital; 46 days since I graduated medical school; 38 days since the murder of George Floyd; 35 days since Israel re-announced plans to annex the West Bank. 500 thousand lives have been lost to coronavirus. The world seems to be a never-progressing, ice-cap melting, scary place.

Florida has set a state-record for increased cases in a single day for twenty-five consecutive days; today with 10,109 new reported cases for a total of 169 thousand cases and 68 new deaths for a total of 3,718 deaths. In Tampa 1,944 new cases were reported for a total of 9,130 cases and 15 new deaths for a total of 132 deaths.

Still the fight for Justice everywhere continued; the protests prevailed; voices kept shouting and screaming; people continued to give generously, recklessly, hopefully. How the human spirit persists I may never know; when all feels meaningless, when reality itself is abysmal, the human mind continues to hope for a world of Justice, and kindness, and opportunity. The mind continues to believe in a reality better than this one, and a version of themselves which is far more than the reality of our daily character.

Call it Values, or Plato's Forms, or Allah, Evolution, Yahweh, Ohm, or the thousand other Gods called upon daily; somehow the human mind believes and persists. And sometimes that hope feels like the morning sun rising courageously and confidently or like the ocean waves crashing recklessly and fearlessly. And sometimes that hope disappears; sometimes it slips away like the dew drop on a scorched summer lawn. Sometimes that hope is stifled like the lingering summer storm whose clouds weigh heavy in the muggy air but never enough to rain. Nevertheless, somewhere deep in the DNA of humanity sits a persisting strength, a resilience which perhaps beats along with the heart, and as imperceivably as breadth itself.

Today would be the beginning of my career as a doctor; the first day I could introduce myself as Doctor Hernandez. This was the beginning of the dream for which I had worked through four years of college and four years of medical school. This was the dream of my lifetime. And twenty-seven years felt like a lifetime to hold a dream.

July 2nd, 2020

Just a few minutes before morning sign out,
I walk the hallways to check my patients,
that they made it through the night.
On the intensive care unit (ICU),
you really never know. The
monotonous beep of every heart
monitor placates my nerves.

They made it through the night,
as did I.

"*Morning sweetheart*" and a smile,
I'm welcomed by
our seasoned nurse practitioner
warrior of the ICU. Burly with
a southern drawl, unfamiliar to
my Northern ears, his full-hearted
laugh would have you thinking
we were anywhere but
an ICU hallway at
the center of
a growing pandemic.

And on morning rounds
his colors came through:
warrior of the ICU,
"This one's fighting, doc. He deserves
a second round of COVID meds."

Remdesivir, a saving drug, was
on national rations.
"We can consider a second
round of dexamethasone...
but Remdesivir we cannot do."

"He's really fighting, doc. Hospital
day 17."

I know he's fighting.
So are all the others who
deserve a life-saving drug.

July 5th, 2020

U.S. 2,902,359 // 129,889
Brazil 1,603,055 // 64,867
Russia 680,283 // 10,145
India 673,165 // 19,268
Peru 302,718 // 10,589

At 5pm a summer storm hit.
The hallways darken as
the summer sun is lost
behind full, crashing rain drops
clouding our hospital windows.
I see the palm trees dance
whipping through the wind.

While the world outside
Screeches through a summer storm,
Our hospital windows silence
the rain as nothing changes
from the inside.
And I wonder if
the world outside changes
so quickly, why not
our hospital world inside?

I don't meet my patients.
It's too high a risk. They say, to limit exposure,
one doctor
sees the patient
every day.
one doctor.
one.
Who is not me.

I type in the orders
attendings ask me to type
Sign. Submit.
I struggle to keep up
with their flying pace.
As though they don't realize
I have to type. Sign. Submit.
Everything they say.

Type. Sign. Type.
Submit.
Type. Sign. Type.
Submit.

I never met
my patients.
It's too high a risk.

730pm. I walked outside for
the first time since morning.
My neck cracked, stiff from
computers and charting,
sore from the weight of my
overstuffed White Coat.
My neck cracked as I looked
straight upwards.

The day was dusk, gone with
the steps I had run
up and down hallways
and stairwells to the beat of
the heart monitor's monotony.

My neck cracked as
I looked upwards to the sky,
missing that warmth of summer
sun's rays, blush on my cheek.

A raindrop fell,
from the cloudless, sunset
sky. And it streamed down my cheek
like a tear from nowhere. And I could
be anyone, or anything, walking out
those hospital doors.

I was an intern, and
I would return with the dawn.

But I could be anyone;
any resident, from anywhere
in the world. Unknown,
unnoticed, replaceable.

July 10th, 2020

U.S. 3,189,117 cases 133,749 deaths
Brazil 1,755,779 cases 69,184 deaths
India 793,863 cases 21,694 deaths
Russia 712,863 cases 11,000 deaths
Peru 319,646 cases 11,500 deaths

I am a healer.
Repeat after me:
I am a healer.

I came home every
evening, after
the sun had set.

I came home every
evening, like
an emptiness after
the life had drained
through me.

I came home every
evening to
a home. He cooked
fresh dinner and waiting
to eat together.

I came home every
evening to
a lover who
embraced my empty body
and filled my lungs
with fresh air.

July 13th, 2020

U.S. 3,369,273 135,324
Brazil 1,884,967 72,833
India 878,254 23,174
Russia 732,547 11,422
Peru 330,123 12,054
Chile 317,657 7,024
Mexico 299,750 35,006
U.K. 290,133 44,830
South Africa 287,796 4,172
Iran 259,652 13,032
Spain 255,953 28,406
Pakistan 251,625 5,266
Italy 243,230 34,967
Saudi Arabia 235,111 2,243

At 12:11PM the overhead speaker announced: "Code Blue, Three West." She repeated, "Code Blue, Three West."

Shit. I started my stopwatch and saved the patient note I was writing in the back office of Three West, the intensive care unit of a community hospital in Tampa Bay. Already wearing a sealed N95 mask, I grabbed my glasses, goggles, face shield, and gown and opened the office door to a rush of providers running down the central hallway; I joined the scurry.

Inside the room laid a 47-year-old woman. She had been admitted to the ICU for severe COVID pneumonia. CPR had been started; I looked at my timer: one minute and 27 seconds had passed since her heart had stopped beating. The respiratory therapist stood at the head of the bed; two nurses alternated chest compressions. Nurses in the hallway mixed vital medications and passed them carefully into the room. The door was shut to limit exposure of aerosolized virus. The attending physician stood outside the glass, giving specific orders every minute.

"Three minutes give first dose epi," he shouted through the glass.... another three minutes past with continued CPR. "Pulse check...," "Dose epi...," "Continue CPR." The cycle went on.

"I think it's a pulmonary embolism" my attending muttered to himself. "...her lips are blue. The\novel coronavirus has been shown to increase a person's risk of blood clots; a pulmonary embolism can be a life-threatening blood clot within the lungs. "Order tPA! STAT! Mix it on their way!" he shouted at me. I turned to the nearest computer and inputted his exact orders while pulling out the phone to call pharmacy.

The charge nurse kept record of every medication given at what time. In a low tone she stated, "We have to save her.... she's me!" She pointed at others in the hallway, "She's you! She is all of us! She's a teacher in her 50's." I looked over her shoulder, her clipboard quivered in her grip; it had been nearly 17 minutes. 17 minuets without a heartbeat.

A pharmacist appeared, running down the hallway with tPA medication in hand, premixed in a small glass bottle. She handed it carefully through to the nurses within the room. We all watched as Mike, a tattooed and pierced nurse I had met that morning, hung the tPA on the IV pole next to an indistinguishable number of medications, attached it to tubing, let the blood clot busting medication drip into our patient's arm. CPR continued amongst rounds of epinephrine pushes and pulse checks.

At the thirty-minute mark, my attending called it, "Time of death, 13:41." Her heart monitor flatlined, and the beeping of her many monitors were silenced one by one. The respiratory therapist covered her exposed body, but not before I saw her bright red chest, rubbed raw from chest compressions. I knew her chest and breasts would turn blue over the subsequent hours as blood settled around ribs broken by CPR. Her fingers and toes were purple from lack of oxygen. Her face was swollen, with open sores along her cheekbones marking the pressure points of the ventilator mask she wore for two weeks.

Mike closed her eyes just as I heard her family arrive on the floor. Seeing our expressions, her husband shouted in agony as he collapsed onto the floor in the middle of the hallway. Visitors had not been allowed into the hospital since the first wave of coronavirus except for end of life.

Every staff member had been pre-fitted with special masks and gowns as to ensure our safety inside COVID+ patient's rooms; the same cannot be done for guests, who under no circumstances were allowed into patient's rooms. Our patient's daughter ran past her father, now pounding his fists on the ground, and slammed her body against the door of her mother's room. She shouted at her mother to wake. She shouted at the nurses to let her inside. She begged, and swore, and cried to feel her mother one last time. Tears streaming down his face, Mike held the glass door closed from the inside, intent on not letting this virus infect even one more person.

I walked down the hallway. A technician had approached the husband, attempting to scoop him off the floor in an embrace. I sunk into the back office, closing the door on the sorrow which had enveloped our ICU floor, and reopened my patient note. I had five more patients to check in with, medication lists to review, billing to complete. Typing away ICD codes, I barely noticed my coffee had gone cold.

July 17th had been the fifth day in a row our hospital ICU had a morning Code Blue for a COVID patient whose heart stopped beating. Some of them were young, like this patient or younger. Some of them were older. Most had been on ventilators. All had COVID pneumonia, and all of them died. Every single patient who had been on a ventilator for COVID pneumonia had died. My patient was one of 128 Floridians to die of COVID on July 15th, with nearly 14 thousand new confirmed cases and nearly 9 thousand hospitalizations throughout the state.

Ben sits at
the first computer,
of the nursing station:
warrior of the ICU,
from his perch
he watches over
both long hallways.

Ben's voice is loud, drawling, husky
you can hear him down
both long hallways.

I hear Ben on the phone,
with his patient's son.
Ben's voice starts to crack,
his patient is not doing better,
quite the opposite. I turn to see
one large tear fall down his cheek
as Ben tells this son his father
is dying,
has been dying all week. "We have
done everything we can" I hear Ben plead.
"But your father is in so much pain,
and there is nothing more
we can do."

Ben pleads with this very son
every day for weeks because
lifesaving measures prolong pain
without signs of recovery,
and every additional measure we take
causes a complication. But this son
refuses to give up. This son thinks he should
not give up on his father when
his father's body has given up
weeks ago.

I hear Ben cry
at the nursing station,
warrior of the ICU
with tears for the suffering
he sees in his patient.

Another Code Blue
another crash cart
Another day
feeling ribs break
beneath the hands of
my chest compressions.

Her ribs rattled
and all I could think
of was a rattle snake
tail. How my patient
deserved poison-a quick,
and painless death-over
this ICU bed of
never ending
measures
to
stave
off
the
undoubtable,
irrevocable
truth
of
death.

And I wondered if
my hands would ever forget,
if my hands would ever
forgive myself
for breaking the ribs
of an 87-year-old
lady
whose body told us
she wanted to
die in peace.

And just like the rest
we called time of death.
And returned to rounds.

I looked down the hallway, and
jumped at the
fleeting sight of
the Husband
flailing on the floor
his fists pounding,
his wails reverberating and
I felt his anger raise
the hairs on my arms.

I blinked and he was gone,
a flit of light, a spark of
memory, and I looked
to my arms, the goosebumps
told me, my body remembered.

Would the ghosts of my patients'
and the wails of their families
ever leave my memory? Would I
wake some five years in my future to
the sight of the Husband
grasping at this ICU floor?

Was he a part of me now?

July 17, 2020

U.S. 3,649,718 138,994
Brazil 2,046,328 77,851
India 1,003,832 25,602
Russia 758,001 12,106
Peru 341,586 12,615
South Africa 337,594 4,804
Chile 326,439 8,347
Mexico 324,041 37,574
U.K. 293,239 45,233
Iran 269,440 13,791
Spain 260,255 28,420
Pakistan 259,999 5,475
Saudi Arabia 245,851 2,407
Italy 243,967 35,028

I picked up dinner on my drive home. I stepped inside to a full house—every table booked by a family or group of friends. All eating, sharing food, breathing in this stale indoor air. All it would take is one person with coronavirus infection breathing in this room to theoretically infect many of the guests. And yet they laughed, mouths wide open and heads thrown back, with no care or concern at all. Waiters wore masks as they rushed to and from tables. Didn't they hear the news; didn't they know people were dying; didn't they know it could be them? I ran out with my takeout in hand and my heart started beating, fast. As I got into my car, I removed my mask, sprayed aerosolized hand sanitizer into the air creating a sheet of mist which encased me. My heart continued beating, now I could feel it in my fingertips as my body began to overheat. My breath quickened as I coughed, breathing in the harsh sanitizer. How could people go on like nothing was wrong? It felt like the indifference and downright ignorant stupidity was undoing the sacrifices for which every healthcare worker bore day after day. I heard their laughs amplified in my eardrums, and it began to feel like the restaurant-goers were laughing at me; laughing at my scrubs, my work, my sacrifice. My breathing slowed and I finally drove home, with a sense of anger and insignificance towards what felt like fighting a war that half the state refused to acknowledge.

Ms. Esperanza, my hope,
intubated for two weeks
pulled her tube right out her throat.
Her heart stayed steady,
her saturation stayed high.

An ICU doc once told me,
if you aren't having self-extubations
on your floor, your patients are too snowed,
your floor too medicated into their unconscious stupors.

Her streak of liveliness
gave me hope. Gave the whole floor hope.
Maybe she will be the one. The one to survive.

Another Code Blue.
Another one.

He'd been dying for days,
his body rejecting every
intervention we provided.
I called his son,
"I am sorry sir, to bring you this news.
I think you should come to the hospital as
soon as possible..."

Guests were not allowed. It was too high a risk.
The exception was imminent death:
the final farewell.

"No" he said.
"I can't come in. Do everything you can."

I needed to be clear. I needed to know
this son understood.

"Sir, I am so sorry. I don't think your father
is going to make it. If you want
to say goodbye, you should come as
soon as possible."

Anger responded, "You call me every day,
to tell me my father is dying. And I tell you
every day
I
want
everything
done."

"I hear you, sir. And I am so sorry. You should never
have to make such a decision. But I need you to know,
your father is in so much pain. He cries when
we lighten the sedation. *We have done*
everything we can possible do...
At this point *there is nothing more we can do.*
We recommend comfort measure,
to ensure your father is not in pain.

Silence met me. Death met me. And the son,
well, the son never met me.

and he never came
to give his father,
whom he so sternly fought for,
a final
goodbye.

And it made me wonder,
who we are really
treating? If we were
treating my patient
he would not have died in pain,
alone and without the son
who could not face
the ugly picture we saw every day.

July 21st, 2020

He stopped counting.
I couldn't bear to look at the numbers either.

After twenty minutes of resuscitation, I called time of death. The respiratory therapist removed the pads holding the ventilator in place on his face, to reveal three black eschars on his pale cheeks each like a rusty penny—ulcers from the pressure of the ventilator he needed to breath for three weeks. His face was puffy with deep violaceous bruising under his eyes. We had put tampons in both his nostrils the night prior as his nose would not stop bleeding from the blood thinners which were required to keep the machine used for his renal replacement from clotting off. He had lost so much weight I could almost see where his ribs had broken from chest compressions. The air of his room was thick and festered. I heard his son's voice inside my own head, exaggerated and shouting, "I tell you every day I want *everything* done." If only he had known what *everything* looks like or smelt like. Maybe then he wouldn't want his father to suffer of *everything* done.

This is the dream,
I said to myself every
morning on my dark
drive to the hospital.
This is the dream
for which I toiled
through four years
of medical school.

This is the dream I
held for a lifetime:
to finally be
doctor.

This is the dream,
I said every morning
to the rising sun. And I
liked to think she shined upon me.

This was the dream,
but it felt tired, ugly
and weary, like the bruising of
my patients faces from
weeks of a ventilator.

Esperanza started to become more ill. The four days of breathing on her own fatigued her 67- year-old body. It was a difficult decision which attendings discussed for 35 minutes before finally deciding to re-intubate her. She needed the ventilator so her body could keep fighting.

I walked into her bedside: capped, gloved, gowned, masked, goggled, feeling more like a medical device than a person. I brought her a warming blanket prior to re-intubation.

She opened her eyes but saw straight through me: she was hungry for air, gasping for breath. I saw the fear glassed over her wide and weary eyes. Alone.
I took her hand in mine; she was ice cold and stiff. "Señora Esperanza", I whispered, and her gaze shifted, finally finding mine. Her breathing slowed as she smiled. "You have to keep fighting. We are doing everything we can. You are our hope."

I had one mask in a baggy for the whole week. The straps are too tight. I feel the pimples growing under my nose. I feel my breath circulated, safe inside my mask. Safe, but hot, sticky, claustrophobic.

I refuse to see the patient without the N95
mask for which I was fitted.
The PPE czar could not find a small duck bill that
morning on her cart. I can't see
the patient. I refuse.

Guilt rose inside my chest, and
I could hear my heart beating in
my eardrums. I signed an oath to
do no harm; who knew how hard it would
become to do no harm unto
myself. How hard it would become to protect myself.

I refused, as I thought of my mother's smile
some three thousand miles away.
I refused, as I looked down the hallway and
saw my ghost: the Husband
who is pleading and shouting on the ICU floor.

Fear walks the hallway.
I see it in everyone's eyes.
I never thought I would refuse to see
a patient. My patient.

I do not know how long
it takes to make a mask,
or a gown, or a face shield.
I do know how long it takes
to make a doctor.

I do not know how much
it costs to make a mask,
or a gown, or a face shield.
I do know how much it costs
to make a doctor, a nurse, a pharmacist.

My patient was full code, but I overheard
her phone call with her boyfriend,
"I just want to die in piece."

"Ms. Case, I know you are in pain. I know
you are scared. Do you want us to resuscitate
you if your heart stops?

No.

"Do you want us to intubate you, if
you stop breathing?"

No. I want to see
my family. I want to
see my boyfriend. I want to leave.

I changed her from full code
to Do Not Resuscitate,
Do Not Intubate. And I called hospice so that she may
leave the hospital to die
in peace with
her boyfriend and her family.

When the hospice workers arrived to
transport Ms. Case, she refused and
I heard her screams from down
the hallway. I walked to meet
her and peered in from the doorway,
the hospice transporters lined up
against the wall.

"Ms. Case, we discussed this is
what you wanted."

No.

I saw the fear in eyes, "Are you sure?"

Yes.

The hospice transporters left and
I switched her back to full code.

I knew my attending would question my
inability to maintain this patient's mind.

I asked myself, what else
could I have done. And the picture
of her screaming through the
hallway as the transporters rolled her bed
out the ICU to hospice
cluttered my mind.
I could not bear
the thought.

That night I cried,
full body tears.

For my patient who could
not face death.

For the Husband who wails
in the hallway—my ghost.

For son who could not
say goodbye to his father.
I cried,
full body tears for
the code, the Husband, the son.

I woke disoriented,
My heart started to run
outside my chest at
full pace as I did
not recognizing the white walls
of our still-new apartment.

I felt his back
against mine and I
remembered it was the
wee hours of morning,
before dawn in
Tampa, Florida.

Condensed dew drops
covered my window,
the humid outside air
stifled overnight, never
abating its relentless heat.

I turned over to face
my lovers neck. I counted
the four moles on his
neck, one covered by
his outgrown, black hair.

I snuck my hands over his waist
and under, until I felt
every part of skin tremble
awake. And we embraced
in a groggy sleep like a dream.

As my heart slowed and
quickened to his light, sleepy touch
I felt green close in
like the green walls where
we made a home out of chaos.

With every heartbeat
I felt myself again:
the woman who loves
and lives, and excites
in my body and his.

Things which leave my mind at ease:

Knowing where the closest Chapstick is,
brush bristles making their way gently through my hair,
the weight of my body pressed into bed sheets,
the coolness of my mother watering her
garden on a hot summer day,
pigeons cooing,
his breath on my neck in
the middle of the night,
orange blossom scent wafting through the air,
the rhythmic beep of my patients'
heart monitors,
sitting down for lunch before 2pm,
sitting down for lunch at all,
pancakes on a Sunday morning,
incense burning a Holy Benediction.

I walked onto the ICU, my shoulders
weary of the month behind me. This
was my beginning, the first month of
Dr. Ammura Hernandez. And I didn't mind
the bags under my eyes or never
brushing my hair or
the constant feeling of life and death teetering
in the hospital hallways. What I missed was
the smile across my face.

This morning, I walked onto
the ICU with a smile. Knowing it was
my last day of these COVID-marked hallways,
the last day of morning code blues before
I had coffee, the last day of patients who
I'd never get to meet but treated through a
computer screen. It would not be the last
time I called a family with difficult news or
the last time I did not have sufficient personal
protective equipment.

This morning I walked
onto the ICU with a smile—
a long, forgotten smile.

Can you sign for the new dose,
hun.
I heard the nurse ask
Of course, I respond with
a smile.

Good morning, sir
Morning sweetheart,
I heard my new patient say.

Sweet like, the full, hot tears of
my patient's suffering, like
the four hours of reading
on my patient's abnormal
presentation. Like,
the four years of undergraduate and
four years of medical school
and
countless sleepless nights for every
exam
Sweet like,
the sugar added to my coffee
to keep my body going.

Sweet like the pomegranate
hanging from my father's tree
broken open at
the end of fall:
grown through scalding
summer days and
patient by his
tender care.

It's not sweetheart,
It's doctor, sir.

The next day I
Self-cared-Sunday:
Ignored emails, mac n cheese in
bed, bath salts and tea tree oil, wore
a t-shirt and nothing else. I
pretended I didn't have three loads
of laundry waiting or a full dishwasher. Pretended
I didn't see patients whose lives ticked
across my memory like a clock. I opened the windows when
the storm rolled in and danced free with the rain. I remembered
what it was to be within these four walls of my body, like being nothing to no one but everything
to me. Just for one day.

I heard Ms. Esperanza died, after two Code Blues in two days. She upheld our in-house statistics of 100% morbidity in patients who were intubated for COVID pneumonia. Though the start of my intern year was the culmination of years of study, meant to launch me into doctorhood, it felt like the end.

Twenty-seven years of my life had brought me to the first day of my doctoring, and no one could have prepared me for the great burden of it all. It felt like living out eschatology which theologians study from their Ivory Towers of the world coming to its final days; like what mad men preach from their city corners. Despite the many hands of patients' I held, the laughs and tears I shared with colleagues, and even the bridges my love built at home with my partner, I felt utterly and completely alone. I felt both like the Husband flailing on the ICU floor and like an empty unknown intern in a forgotten computer room: helpless at the inevitability of Death.

The dream I held was all together realized and shattered as I could barely hold all the pieces of my patients, my passions, my expectations, my relationships together in my own body. Medical school had taught us a thousand ways to heal a patient and cure a body. The novel coronavirus laughed at the falsity of our medical superiority complex, showing the glaring failures of our healthcare system and society at large. There was no scientific textbook or eschatological theory, or belief system that could prepare us—the healthcare workers—for the sheer volume of lives lost, nor the weight of it all.

Every avenue of healthcare—from personal protective equipment, to social distancing and mask-wearing mandates, to drugs and vaccines—was politicized, commercialized, and lost in a sea of misinformation and what we were left with was dying patients in fear-filled hospital hallways, with families who would never recover, and healthcare workers who would never forget and perhaps never heal from the suffering born in death.

The end of the summer marked one million deaths by coronavirus, globally; the United States claimed two hundred thousand of them. Epidemiologists and biostatisticians estimated that number could double by the end of 2020. For those of us on the front lines, the distressing sense of uncertainty became the new norm. A great chasm was created between those of us who felt the weight of coronavirus and those who remained willfully unaware. The world persisted in what felt like the end times and life, love, and death were found together, every day during the time of coronavirus.

Ammura **Hernandez** is a resident physician. She completed her intern year in internal medicine and is continuing her residency training in psychiatry. As a graduate of Scripps College and the George Washington University School of Medicine, she is passionate about the intersections of medicine, humanities, diversity, and social change. *An Eschatological Isolation* is her debut collection of poetry. Her poetry and writings have been published in *Harmony Magazine, Medpage Today, in-House, The Human Touch Journal, Hektoen International Journal of Medical Humanities, The Medical Student Press Journal,* and *In-Training,* where she also served as an editor. You can follow her ongoing work @thepoetdoc.

Author Contact:
Ammura Hernandez MD
ammura.hernandez@gmail.com

www.ingramcontent.com/pod-product-compliance
Lightning Source LLC
Chambersburg PA
CBHW021148090426
42740CB00008B/996